THEY CURVE

LIKE

SNAKES

First Printing: 2021

Paperback ISBN: 978-1-952869-50-1

Cover Photo by Julie McFarland
Cover Art & Design by C. M. Tollefson
Editing by C. M. Tollefson & Airea Johnson

Cathexis Northwest Press

cathexisnorthwestpress.com

THEY CURVE
LIKE
SNAKES

a collection of poems by
David Alexander McFarland

Cathexis Northwest Press

THEY CURVE LIKE SNAKES

a collection of poems by

David Alexander McFarland

Concrete Wolverine Press

For Julie, Alexander, and Camille

As for you, O Lord,
you will not restrain
your mercy from me.

Bodies eating bodies, heads eating heads,
we are nothing eating nothing,
and though we feast,
are filled, overfilled,
we go famished.

Table of Contents

Blood in the wood

There's blood in the wood outside my door,
a spot of darkness in any light, there because
I cut myself, but still I had to let the dog come in.
I bled around the pressure through the napkin,
grinding teeth against that millennial memory—
the feel of steel sliding through easy flesh—
while cursing all knives and my foolishness.
A little numbness still persists.
Painful miscalculation—
the history of my life.
Scars accumulate,
memories grow.

Paris

Nothing to do sits heavy in me. Oh,
laundry to wash and fold, hallways to mop,
dusting and errands, yards to keep up
wait for me—and soon snow to shovel plus
salt to spread like Millet's sower to save me
from falling again on my hip and shoulder
which hurt for months after. *After*.

Now is *after*.
Energy was *before*.
Before blood pressure,
cholesterol,
bad sleep,
bad feet,
age.

Energy was purpose,
a showing of daffodils
in a dead yard.

I dream of walking miles in Paris.

The ordinary wearies,
but there's nothing else.

Trains

In the night sometimes we talk of trains,
saying how there ought to be more,
high speed like the one from Paris
to Angoulême, to compete with the airlines,
get some cars and trucks off the roads.

From Paris to Angoulême
I saw sunflower fields
out to the horizon—
as in a story book,
a fantasy—
a moment to be savored in memory
like a fine Parisian dinner.

With a great train ride we could be soon in Atlanta,
have all day in Chicago, go west to the Grand Canyon,
maybe all the way to the Golden State
to see if sunsets there really are.

That spring night before my mother's funeral
six trains came slowly through that tiny town,
blowing horns well before and long after—
rocking over old rails, trembling air and ground,
touching every house in town.
Two blocks away, that *son ancien*,
that elemental noise fixed forever in my brain.

Now I hear them
all times of the year,
trains on both sides
of the Mississippi,
sliding through while
horns rising falling
along the bluffs.
And I think of her,
waiting in a funeral home,
me in bed wanting to cry,
too tired to do so.
Too many compacted
moments playing out.
Pacing myself for
that final reunion.

The poppies of France

A Sa Emile Richard, du St. Palais sur Mer, 1888-1912
Disparu en mer du paquebot Titanic 1912
—Plaque in the cemetery in St. Palais sur Mer

The poppies of France fade away,
going to seed on the road to the Super U
in the June sun, their sweetness done—
fading into a memory. Even fading
from that—leaving the common flowers,
all the blues and whites, the yellow,
to persist and sing along the road.

June is hot and good. Poppies
gone to seed make me think
of the death of all plants.
All death. My death.
When I will be no more.

Emile exists no more:
his blood and flesh, his bones
melted in the Atlantic.
The Titanic left him. Lost him.
Twenty-four against my seventy.
Not so great a difference, really.

My grandfather made twenty-seven,
when his appendix lost itself and him.
His marker's weathered away
like bones in the sea.

Emile saw the poppies in his day,
the whites and yellows, the blues.
Blues the color of the water above,
black below.

Really ripe strawberries

Really ripe strawberries from my yard
bleed in the summer and taste like love itself.
They overflow containers, get sugared into jam
carefully ladled into jars and capped,
labeled against time with this year's number—
or frozen carefully so frost cannot make me
throw out in winter what I want to remember.

Snow on glass

While I waited for coffee,
a snowflake hit my window
and melted down. A big flake,
one so large I could see its
radial arms, the fingers on each arm.
Perfect, perfectly formed, I said,
(as if my review counted for anything)
focusing without my glasses—
nearsightedness a blessing now,
with nothing between me and
what is but the glass on which
it lay supine. *Like every picture
I've seen*. Like every picture in books,
blown-up, perfect Internet images,
more perfect than any plastic
Christmas tree resemblance.
On the glass it persisted
for that moment. The arms,
each finger stretched out—
maybe those melted first.
Which makes me think of time
intervals, that instance between one
clock tick, the next. How long
that can last when one is conscious
of a clock having ticked at all. We
don't have that now: instants are digital,
smoothly shown in moving hundreds,
thousands and so on. But what is
between one square wave and
the next, the next, the next...
Really, all seemed to alter
together, contracting, turning
transparent, staying for one
more instant liquid in the
original pattern. Until gravity
made it sag like an old man's
belly before all returned
to what was.

Sleeping in Paris

Where her soul has gone
I cannot know. Her ashes
sleep in Paris, all about her
courtyard, a bright little square
of careful plants. It's easy to
think of her living there still—
the solace I need to imagine that
bright face, to hear the easy laugh,
the quiet voice spilling over
with memories and plans
for the rest of her truncated life.

I would have been her lover
if she had wanted me,
but it was never so.
She would have left me
and I might have turned
bitter as many do. Still,
I keep the memory of her
stored away in my brain
where she lives still
in perfection, loved by me,
finally, all alone.

Lost

Between my *here* and *there*,
one little step, the next,
I lost the thought that put
my feet in motion. Oh,
a little word, a simple
request displaced the thought
so wonderful, marvelous
that said get up, put down
a line, make a story
a poem, get something to save
a sparkling thought just
now burnt out, which left
its ash in these few lines.

They curve like snakes

They look like old dead snakes that might come out
to lie on grass to die–not in some decent
hiding place. Brown twists that curl and give a start
of sudden moves but never move across
the tops of grass but falling when the wind
shakes up the hill. The old catalpa trees
are dirty trees, a nasty tree that litters
streets and yards with pseudo-snakes that cause
a stop a freeze to seize myself to see
that curve, a little spasm in adrenaline
to surge towards my feet, to make me run
to run before I see the curve is not
a movement after all but just a cracking
silent fibrous husk that once had been
so green: a snake-like long enough to have
that flickering tongue to taste the air while searching
out another meal. The seeds do that,
the growing up in flower beds, in lawns,
in cracks of sidewalks, anywhere a little soil,
the chance at life, a solitary life
that cares not where its seeds may go but that
they grow up and compete for light and air and rain,
for age that grows and twists the trunks.
They curve like old snakes in my lawn
to scare me in a senseless moment,
when I am not thinking where
my feet might go or how it is to find
a twisting moving shadow through the grass
as frightened as me but safe and gone
before I have the chance to find myself.

The second of April

Spring announces itself in wind that
swirls leaves in little tornadoes, blows
over the recycling cart. Paper, cans
and plastic seem to have lives, swimming
boldly away from their confinement.
Already the power's out.
The fridge is warming,
the house cooling,
windows rattling, unnerving
us both, making us snappish.

At the top of the hill, in the open,
frozen leaves rush together,
rush toward a common destination.
So many escaped the rakes, the sacks,
composters, burning—coming out of ravines,
ditches, yards where people could not or
would not manage them last fall—
the old or ill, the lazy, or those overwhelmed
by the Herculean task. The stop sign waggles to
everyone. Greeting or warning,
I cannot tell.

There's warmth in the car, a rocking in the gusts—
somewhat pleasant. I could be lulled to sleep by it
in the afternoon when my body's want overcomes
my desire. Warm sun in the window, a murmuring
almost below my hearing, plus a bit of rocking
can make me young again every day.

Flood season

The Mississippi rides among the trees,
silent as nuns at a funeral, engulfs its
smaller islands, eroding, dumping
sand and silt contaminated with
farm runoff, leaves and sticks from
Illinois and Wisconsin, Minnesota,
fish trapped when retreat sounds.
Snow melt pushes dirty water over parks,
into living rooms, wallboard, around
foundations, against sandbags where
someone with experience ordered them.
Floods always seem a discordant symphony
of wills combating—time always declares
a draw. Water retreats and streets get hosed,
sighs released, repairs begun or houses
demolished while lessons learned we hope
are written down for another tough spring.

I've stood in its mouth,
let its clear water run over
my bare feet, held my
children's hands as they
fearfully crossed—it wasn't
so bad, not dangerous or
extra slippery. So, laughing,
they went back and forth
with all the bravado of
the very young. And the water
ran down the hill from
Lake Itasca into the trees,
the very image of all the
things one cares to assign.
I choose only to think
of the river's beginning,
and nothing more.

Wind

The October wind blows
like a lover who is leaving,
not in a huff but resolutely,
showing you how much
you will miss her warmth—
how cold the house will be.

23 January

December snow
is gone today
from yards, roads,
the muddy brown
and black edges
of roads cleared.
Black clots from cars,
smelted snowmen whose
metal proved false—
all gone even from
the sheltered places.
Fifty degrees yesterday
finished the job.
Global warming's
real this January.
Uncovered winter ground
seems ugly-browned,
more alive with corruption
than promises of green,
no sight nor smell
of spring, no hope
which ought to
replace snow.

Spring is heavy on the world

for Sidney

Spring is heavy on the world
today, but I am looking,
seeing how her skin's
become transparent,
how it has a fine Chinese
ceramic finish, wondering
how and why her veins got smaller.

Spring is heavy on the world,
and she is panting, trembling,
standing limp with effort,
turns on thick feet–going
five feet, back, and drops
into her wicker chair
to smile and says,
How lovely, sweet the breeze is.

Spring is heavy on the world,
and I am…I am thinking
nursing home…a burial program
while the sweetly perfumed,
lovely morning washes over
me. So. I am thinking of erosion.

Last day of November

Today could be spring, late March.
Thirty-four degrees, no wind,
rain dripping from trees and
everywhere, breath visible,
rising before vanishing.
Gray midwestern sky
reaches over the Mississippi,
stretches over Iowa.
The day's a promise.
But every day's a promise.
In March I will be
thinking planting, deciding
what and where.
Now it's winter,
cold air in my house,
snow and salt.
Too late for us to fly south.
The children have roosted,
feathering their nests
against needs and wants,
against their future.
They know no more
than I those years ago.
I breathe, sigh,
breath vanishes.

Students in English 101

They all write in present tense.
"I want to be impactful," they say,
meaning *immediate, strong, vivid.*
Or do they mean *to be exciting.*
They just don't know how to be
what they want in this moment,
this class, these years, this life.
Not yet. Give them thirty years,
let them fall into and out of jobs,
marriages, affairs, and they might
learn to value the verbs that mark
their time, the order of memory.

A birthday gift

Made in China the cup reads.
All celebrates Paris, le Metro,
patisserie, poppies, outdoor cafés.
This is the world we have now.

No doubt the gift is to remind her
of the places she's been,
the good times
getting expresso in cafés,
standing at the foot
of the Tower,
the Arc de Triomphe,
photographing
while remembering
Germans in war films
marching through.
Today, there's only traffic
with con men preying
on tourists, cursing
when one fails
to fall into the trap.

Travel's a trap,
Jefferson said,
"its recollection poisons..."
Maybe he's right. Still.
I long for Paris,
travel, new smells, or
a Loch Ness monster.

Ageing

An oil change is not simple nowadays.
I used to do it with a wrench, a pan.
Now someone pokes and prods,
measures and computes from codes,
examining all the ways age and wear have
brought down performance, worn away
protective surfaces, strained a linkage,
makes recommendations, strongly suggests
replacement parts. *Here's what we can do for you.*
There ought to be something better.

At the end I get a good bath, soap and a rinse,
scrubbed and waxed, blown dry,
and we're out in the sun for a romp,
a bit of shopping to show ourselves off,
waiting for a little whistle,
an appreciative smile
we're too old for.

October storm

So fall has come, finally.
Riding behind a good storm
that sent us to the basement
with emergency lights, thinking
about the past storms full of lightening,
high winds. We watched water come in,
crawl over the floor like a chilled snake,
undulating over concrete until exhausted,
relaxing to fall into a dark pool before
it reached us. More house repairs coming.

We slept till seven, fifty-two degrees.
A good fall sleep even in the damp.
Coffee, the ordinary concerns
of another day carried out in
the gray day, the damp day
that in the Midwest may or not
mean more rain. Moisture from Texas,
the Gulf, from Canada, whatever our
world's rotation sends.

All I know is what the weather map shows,
Green for light rain, yellow and red for danger,
down the stairs, pray a little, hope for the best.
Savor the morning, bless the coffee in the damp,
the coolness, look at the limbs and leaves on
the lawn. Call the children, check on them.

The color of your heart

Is it white like virgins, a deep new snow
on Saturday morning? New white linen
still creased from the package, fresh
white like nurses' uniforms from the old days
before colors allowed them to fade
and be just like everyone else.
Like the light that shone brightly in that
moment of your meeting for the first time.

Is it black as a rainy night with clouds
that block the moon, the stars? Streetlights
so gone in the storm to suggest deeds hidden
and only whispered into confidential ears.
Dark as a grievance held decades long and
still frustrated. Like the grave that opened
when your love slammed the door and
never will again.

Has your heart come a dark, bloody red?
A stop sign unheeded until the crash.
Shiny red like a fire engine slicked with rain
and racing to the scene, or a Chinese red
that should have carried you both through
to the end but failed centuries ago.
The red-hot anger that was all the inheritance left
when that door slammed shut with its eternal noise.

Has it turned as blue as the Pacific might have been
when Magellan sailed upon it for the first time?
Blue as before the world started,
the April sky after a warming rain,
cleansed to a robin's egg.
Just that shade of blue that bespeaks serenity
after your long introspection—deciding it was
truly all your fault, though your heart's beat's regulated
by a well-remembered din that never fades.

Corpse

That thing's been dead for days;
the city hasn't picked up the corpse
that's sat in the summer sun,
bloated, deflated, grew armies
of flies that bred again.
Can't tell what it was,
raccoon, possum—
not skunk.
Not from the bits of fur
still clean of the blood,
browns that change
each time I drive past.

Water

Hands in the sink,
I wait in the flow,
wishing, remembering
the cold of January,
February, but June
has warmed the ground
too deep. This moment,
I miss the frost
that reached far down,
that made ice in a glass
unnecessary—not that
I want even a momentary
return of cold that
makes knees ache,
toes and fingers numb,
when I feel mortality
eating me from the inside.
My thought leads
from *here* to *there*.

On hearing the worst news

On a bright Rochester day
the juice came out of the apple,
the orange got squeezed so dry—
the lemon's bitterness burns.
This car's out of gas,
coasting to a stop somewhere
close. Sweet words are hard to find.
Bitterness wants to flower like
goldenrod or oppress the way
Saharan heat desiccates the unwary.
No one comes truly prepared.

Normal

Normal changes with every disease—
now it's pills for diarrhea, nausea,
abdominal pain, and all the little things
that promise aid for that day's great misery,
learning how far ahead to take what.
Daily pills rest on the floor under the table
because there I remember them, can
reach them without having to rise from
my chair; emergency pills—atropine,
imodium and more—stay in the backpack
with clean pants, diapers and shields,
those necessary things when there's
an explosion. In my suitcase some extra
cannabis gummies stay, and she keeps
the oxy in her purse so I don't overdose
in pain. Nothing is where it would have
been among vitamins, cholesterol pills,
cold remedies in the medical cupboard.
Convenience wars with necessity.
Something's always easy to reach,
but routines alter,
habits transmute.

Second cycle

On the road north, I listen to
Bareilles moaning beautifully,
"Stay tonight," to a lover going,
and Joni croons in an
old fashioned way how she wants
to be in love again
while wipers bite back
against the intermittent drops.
The skies north stay gray,
and I wonder if we ought
to be gray ourselves.
Last trip up north,
rain beat at us going up
and back, flailed and rocked us
hard. I felt cleansed. Now here's
two hundred fifty pleasant miles
to talk of ourselves, and even
our talk of bad days
can make us smile
just a little.

On treatment day, from the seventh floor
grey clouds move slowly on the ridge of trees.
Even grey clouds hold a promise of something.
I wait for my drugs, wait for the evening's
collapse. Up and down like the weather,
the season. A guitar plays in my ear,
someone moans in Spanish,
nurses come and go, check the dripping,
vanish on other business—patients
and paperwork for a vast bureaucracy
always under construction. And the
news comes—everything is running behind,
drugs an hour late, which gets us out of here
an hour later. Supper will be soup tonight.
But lunch is a roast beef sub
while I can still enjoy the taste.

Done, the needle out, bandage wrapped,
shoes on, we can leave the deserted floor—
empty of workers to check people in
for tests or chemo—tomorrow flocks will
wait quietly for their names and a cheery face
at a door. *Tomorrow.* The waiting area
depresses without a constant murmuring,
movement, an occasional odd or exotic outfit,

37

the Mantovani music, a gathering five-thirty
winter gloom in the windows that show
a town headed home. The energy of the day
is vanquished which stays with me
until we too find bright lights and a warm room.

Treatment

Conversations filter in,
fragments of voices
that rise from other
patients, nurses, then
sink to nonsense
mingled with bits of
television shows—
someone close is
watching *Andy Griffith*.

It's not a buzz like
afternoon television.
From my chair that
can lull me to sleep
sometimes. In the
dim light of my cubicle,
nothing really puts
me out—preferable
to the immediate
noise of the iv pump
measuring, counting
down my life
in soft electronic
beeps. I can't read
on my phone;
moving my arm
makes the needle
jab and makes
me anxious again.
Everything makes me
anxious again.
When she comes
to take it out,
fears drain away
like bath water—
hunger and sleep
the only appointments
left in this day.

I 80 west, US 63 north

Glorious blue sky,
with bits of clouds
hanging about, grain
trucks on the road,
anonymous trucks
in white, movers,
package haulers,
oversize Deere tractors,
cement mixers, all
sorts mixed in with
cars that zip past
trucks, create a wind
in grasses, against
sign posts, flowers
that congregate in
ditches for nearly
all my way.

This is the day to travel in,
sunlight bright as memory—
where summer flowers
along the roads bluer
than the sky, more
yellow than finches,
white so clean—
new sheets fresh
out of plastic;
watching saves me
from anxiety about
tomorrow, new chemo
and effects that
might be permanent
like numbness,
vision loss, and those
memories of *before*—
when I was whole.

Body parts

Interesting to have the tips
of my fingers numb all the time;
I check my toes on cold days
to see if they need a warm soak.
My lips tingle from time to time;
my message worries the Clinic staff
enough to call—they think a stroke,
but she says nothing is drooping.
Buttoning is different on some shirts,
and zipping up feels different.
Don't stub a toe, I tell me.
The pain's the same. But the touch
worries me, and kissing isn't the same
I am sure for her as well. If the numbness
worsens, the Clinic will cut back on
the chemo, but do I want that?
Yes and no. Yes and no.

Falling trees

"Two people killed at courthouse,"
all the news people said, dwelling
on the 4th of July tragedy for days,
a week—people watching fireworks
over the river, being innocent
until the moment of the fall.
The county cut down that tree
and more. Blunt force tragedy,
blunt force remedy. It is what
every government does.

When I walked my dog yesterday,
a limb fell not six feet in front
of me, which made me remember
the two dead, feel how I could be
another. But it wasn't so large,
diameter about three inches, split
in the breaking, leaves beautifully green,
summer not yet turned ochre or
crimson for the fall. I laughed
a bit, remembered again,
grew sober.

That limb's just another reminder:
Bukowski's horses run faster than me.
Time and chance happens to them all,
the Preacher says. *Give me time*, Lord,
give me time since chance had its shot
and got me good.

Fading

My rosebuds nearly faded away,
I cannot go to Innisfree, not today
nor next month. Too old, so set
in certain ways. I cannot take a
new place, make small talk
with strangers. My bed is
made and it's comfortable.
Let me die in my old bed
or at least a hospital bed
downstairs, my children
near, my wife in tears.
I won't know.
Let the morphine
slip me into
angel arms
to be made
new again
eternally.

Pain

Pain is not *weakness leaving*
despite what singers and
exercise leaders say; it sucks
away what made me, leaving me
three steps behind truly living.
Biceps will heal, ankle soreness
fades in days, though heartaches
dim over years and decades—
they compost well till stirred by
a voice, a sudden seeing in memory
the face of that loved one gone away
long ago. Tumor pain comes a
storm tide; its highs make me reach
for bottles as it devours a bit more.
Don't mistake pain for
a strength to come.

Going north in December

Going north's always a guess
if skies remain a winter gray—
when all blues and greens transform
to black-and-white; estimates
of distance for me are useless.
Not depressing, really; most
Midwest winter days are gray
from first light to last—grays are
the normal I've grown used to.

Just now the skies toward Rochester are blue,
brilliant with sun and thin strips of clouds,
low traffic counts, twenty-three degrees,
but I brought my warmest coat because
this is Minnesota with its legendary cold.
A rare few corn fields remain for a harvesting;
the storm that dropped twelve inches on us
in Illinois touched nothing here. So brown
grasses, dark trees, empty gray bean fields
line our route, squirrel nests and farmhouses
tucked beside larger white barns; metal silos
glint from far off, on metal covers over concrete
tubes; no doubt all are full of corn and beans.
We whizz past as fast as we dare. Suddenly
the world shows in technicolor, and
color in the day is some promise of more
and more tomorrow, but that promise
comes as variable as the weather.

Chemo brain

Every situation is a state of mind.

A chemo brain takes only one brief
moment to be speeding down
its sturdy rails faster than the TGV's
on a ride which cannot ever be retraced,
going downhill, up again with abandon—
a scene or two dazzles, saved
though they fade soon enough,
confusing nodes that touch
nothing else—and goes on past
the sunflower fields of France in
glorious golden bloom, and I see
the whiteness of Florida shores,
a dark Alabama pine forest,
Illinois' green green corn fields,
never pausing at stations
until I fall asleep or realize
she has called out my name
another time, and I become fixed
once again in what is her world
and once was mine.

Apologies to Sandberg

Pain comes on soft cat feet,
curls up on my lower belly,
waits until its weight becomes
    intolerable
      and
will not move even
when force is used:
    cannabis.
      and
    oxycodone
Insufficient crowbars
to move a fluid weight.

A little pain pill

When I whisper *yes* to her in
my hoarse, my strangulated voice,
yes, please yes to that little white
pill, an oxy to dampen down
those abdominal torments made
stronger with another treatment,
this four day migraine,
backache from too long
nailed to my chair, and all
those ordinary miseries of cancer—
if *normal* is leaving a person
not so much more than
a brittle, thin glass that at
any moment will implode—
I am truly grateful.

Lint

An ugly, gray piece of lint
came out my pocket
stuck to my infused
cherry candy, ugly against
the fake pink color.
With numbed fingers
I could not get it off.
So in it went, ruminated
in all the sweetness meant
to mask the dry and
grassy taste; I tasted
under the sweet a blandness
refusing to unravel
in my sweetened spit,
becoming the only thing
left after the good stuff
went down to fulfill
my need and desire.
Sweet and sticky fingers
looking for some place
to leave the grayness.

Crying

She has seen me cry
too many times,
oh, yes, from the pain,
the constancy, a mean
persistence spreading
upwards from the root
of me until there is no end
to it, added instantly
to all those times before
because the body remembers
and keeps locked away
for later, recalling every pain—
memories constantly renewed.

And I have cried for myself
when I see an end, so I cry
for her, then for family and
friends who pray for me and call,
visit, send cards, who give
hope on the better days.
I cringe before the dark,
remembering the subtractions
throughout my life, parents
and grandparents, a sister,
too many friends, school pals;
afraid of that pain, I cry
even though I know
morphine or another drug
will make you comfortable.
So I might go not knowing
the moment of
my great translation.
I wonder what
I should truly desire.

Let us dance

Let us dance to
this slow and
less-than-pleasant
little tune that's saved
for you and I alone.
Let's dance slowly
for just a little while,
a few minutes at least;
a faster tune
will come along
soon enough,
but a slow one
is best for our
relationship
if that could
be the best term—
word idea *understanding*—
(pick one of the above
or offer me a better one)
for you being under,
in my skin, my blood.
Carefully
please,
because you have
wounded me already,
so much that my belly
aches with you, my mind
clogs like an old toilet in
those hard moments when
standing makes me nearly
scream.

On a better day

I feel better this morning
than yesterday and that
day before when all that time
I spent on the couch or in
my chair, waiting for my
back pain to pass, waiting
for my headache to lift
like a morning's dew in
a hot and dry July;
abdominal pain never dies.
Now my belly might accept
a bit more food and drink—
maybe a whole chicken thigh,
some few ounces of beef.

I do not know how to talk
about feeling better. Bad days
come in their darkling clouds
and when they go the dawning
reveals that swelling dark tide
which will overwhelm me.
Scattering through my memories
I see all my days discolored, darkened.

In Rochester, day before

The world seems in slow motion.
The line of trees beyond the window
seems caught between fall and winter—
the tallest devoid of leaves of any color,
the sheltered, shorter trees' leaves all dark
in the late daylight, the gray, opposed by
the fashionably painted bright buildings nearby.

The light that neither promises rain tonight
nor tomorrow has faded slowly away
by the time we slip into bed to warm up,
to rest and review the plan for tomorrow.
Blood, chemo. Not chemotherapy—too formal.
(I've fallen in with everyone here, shortening
every word possible like a good Midwesterner.
People here always call me Dave).

Another routine like the last: vials of blood,
needles in the arm that I hope will miss
the scar tissue in my veins; I hope for
a terribly skilled nurse who chats amiably
while setting up poisons to plague me
for the next week.

I am in limbo, waiting
for an immediate winter
or some promise of spring.
I cannot calculate the odds.

Six a.m., Rochester

In the dark outside Charlton
the public sidewalk sparkles silver
under florescent lights; a December's
early morning's too cold to admire
the sight more than the time
it takes for me to lean on my cane
and hobble in for my blood letting—
they only take a little but is required.

At nine, in my chair,
chemo needle in,
medicines dripping,
I remember the sparkle,
the sudden beauty
I had to pass by;
sorry I could not stay
and admire more,
show her the little
wonder from every angle,
but saving my life must
remain on schedule..

Energy

When for a briefness—
at sixty, all things slip pass
by in a hurry—the turbines
on the hill lined up in my eyes,
so the blades turned like madmen
in a silent cacophony, one arm
chasing two more, acres of
white blades whirling over
yesterday's snow against a fair
blue sky, obeying their manufactured
nature, nothing more—which
may be a mirror of my days,
the way my chemo brain works
(at best only intermittently well)
before arriving at a satisfying
answer that might strike a spark.

Blue skies

There's no blue sky
like those over empty fields;
slight clouds fade into the rich
blue, and khaki fields plus
white snow makes a stark but
not unpleasant contrast though
I haven't decided about the
empty trees, whether they add
or detract in their starkness.
The clumps of pines seem friendly
enough this close to Christmas,
wind breaks grown full,
plump as turkeys.
But we're past them
all in a hurry, houses,
farms, stands of trees
that have purpose—
set boundaries,
decorate driveways
in green seasons.
Away from the road
I see a stillness
which I know is illusion.
Only the surface is
quiet; all work done,
now a long and cold rest.

Northward

The fields are beautifully green,
corn and beans all the way
to the end of my eye.
Wrens and sparrows wing past
my car, wheeling heedless, and
miss by little inches a windshield
moving north above every speed limit.
Northward the sky promises rain,
but since I cannot forecast anything,
I do not trust the clouds nor me.

My tumor's pain isn't so bad, though;
I'm always aware it's committing suicide,
growing, coming into flower, evading
the danger of a wall moving fast,
obeying its mindless nature:

Fevers

Fevers come and go, low grade, sure,
but must be watched. 100.4 is the line
between emergency rooms or
pills at home. Fevers come after two o'clock.
98.9. We measure, watch, look for a trend.
Drugs. Wait, watch the rapidity of
digital spots, the flashing F to furnish
my answer. By bedtime, relax again. Or not.

In the treatment room, people introduce
themselves like servers who believe
I will remember them tomorrow.
The doctor like the chef waits
for her workers to truss me with two
iv lines, draw vial after vial of blood,
measure and weigh, and finally comes
to see just what can be done with this cooling flesh.

In an hour I chafe at the pace of things
After a lot of blood, ecg, flu test up the nose
that almost reaches my brain, pissing in the cup.
Then no one comes in until the doctor,
who asks things they should have
written down, have saved in all their networks.
Have to ask—have to check.

In three hours I want out, feeling a lifer already.
Temp is down, blankets thrown off, bored.
Can't tell from the wall clock if it's one time
or another—both hands look the same
on the imitation analog face.
Only the second hand gives meaning
that has become meaningless.

At home, all is right. The house still stands,
the dog did not shit on the floor, the bed is
as soft as before, and I sink into it, say a prayer
for deliverance as much as for my future.
The never used iv sites still sting,
one bleeds on my sheet;
the other stings for days.
Pain is instructive, I've heard.
Perhaps it says this time
there are still more days.

Creature comforts

The rattling of our heater
comforting while it rains
outside, while we wait for the
promised snow—at first
we were promised six to nine,
then nine to twelve. Now less
than six. A relief, really. For me.
My son will maybe come
and blow it off the sidewalks,
put down salt, make it clean
so we can get out to the car
to go north on Tuesday—
now the focus of our week.

Few things comfort me.
The heater comforts
and there's still
touch and taste,
the feel of her skin,
smelling chicken soup.
The daily routines,
television shows on
their own schedules.
Tuesdays, Wednesdays—
my treatment days—
have their routines:
blood in vials, go
piss in the cup,
get hooked up for hours
and wait for days to feel
better—something close
to my new normal. We've
waited weeks and months
for uncertain results.
Not much comfort there.

A cancerous life

It's most like walking in summer
sunshine on alga-slippery rocks
knee-high in a fast stream,
negotiating turns, getting past
overhanging, fallen branches,
swift currents that threaten to
put me down into the cold,
subtracting all my heat,
any thoughts or plans,
with all the sudden explosion of
winter wet that wants my complete
surrender to the flow that will
separate all my parts,
push every atom
finally to the sea.

I saw snow in April

I saw some snow in April,
drove through it coming
into town, a whiteout moment
that had her reaching for the
headlight switch, slowing, looking
for that green car in front now
swallowed up. For one moment
we were alone in the whited world,
and then we were past, back in traffic
and color, fully back in the real world
of gray skies, an appointment for chemo,
an evening with an upset belly, a choice
of drugs, including what I brought
across state lines illegally (better
tasting) in an Altoids box and those
stronger ones in our suitcase.
I knew I would sleep in spite
of the little pump attached
at my chest, the string that
I follow to find the bag and
carry it to the bathroom with me.
I hate it when my cord is tugged.

I saw snow in April and later
saw white patches of December,
January not yet moved, transformed
into ground water or filtered away
to the Zumbro River.
I saw snow in April. That little storm
blowing hard—so localized,
started-to-done in two minutes—
stays with me. It ought to mean more,
I say this now, but I can't connect
the snow, its whiteness and the speed
of its going along, the suddenness
of its end—no, I cannot say it's a portent,
a great symbol or just metaphor,
no matter how long I torture my memory.
Never mind.
To possess the memory is enough.

Writing while sick

One more poem, short or long,
sweet or harsh, will make
no difference, no change,
no relief in my awful urgency
for a bathroom, my sudden
irrational hunger for what is
not in the fridge, nor hot and
ready when I am—or as pleasant
as bright sunlight moving across
the wood floor, accurate sundial
until it passes out the window behind.

One more poem will make
no difference to you but it
will fill me up with a good
moment some morning or
afternoon, leaving me with
a little smile, a tiny pleasure
still left to me in the
debris of my days.

Acknowledgements

"A cancerous life." *Cathexis Northwest Press*

"Apologies to Sandberg." *Marathon Literary Review*

"Blood in the wood." *Coe Review*

"Body parts." *Santa Anna River Review*

"Crying." *Cathexis Northwest Press*

"Lost." *The Paumanok Review*

"Really ripe strawberries." *Poem*

"The second of April." *Deep South Magazine*

"They curve like snakes." *Deep South Magazine*

"Trains." *SheliaNoGig Online*

"Wind." *Broad River Review*

David Alexander McFarland was born April 29, 1948 in Shelbyville, Tennessee, but spent most of his childhood in Cullman, Alabama at the Childhaven Children's home run by The Church of Christ. He found refuge in books as a child, and that continued throughout his life, whether he was serving with the Airforce in Thailand during the Vietnam War or working on the line at the Chrysler plant in Alabama. After graduating from the University of Alabama, Huntsville, he went to Iowa to earn an MFA in Creative Writing at the University of Iowa Writers' Workshop. While in Rock Island, Illinois to see UAH professor and mentor H.E.Francis at a local writers' conference, he met Julie Coyne Johnston, and they spent the next 37 years together. He continued to write, mostly short stories, but also a novel, essays, and poetry. He was a "stay at home dad," writing during the children's naps and teaching English and Literature part time at Blackhawk College, Scott Community College, and Augustana College, among others. Upon retirement, he was named Adjunct Professor Emeritus at Blackhawk College. In addition to his life as a reader, writer, and teacher, David was a devout Christian, a bee-keeper, cooking enthusiast, competitive swimming official, fisherman, and music lover.

David Alexander McFarland published essays, fiction and poetry internationally, in print and online. Nominated for The Pushcart Prize, he also was short listed for the Iowa Short Fiction Award and won a Highly Commended citation for the 2020 Bridport Prize in England. He taught at literary workshops, especially those organized by what was to become The Midwest Writing Center. In later years, he concentrated almost exclusively on poetry.

In 2018 David was diagnosed with stage 4 pancreatic cancer, and many of the poems he produced during the two and a half years of his illness were written in the car during the 250 mile drive to Mayo Clinic in Rochester, Minnesota where he underwent cancer treatment. He continued to write well into the final weeks before his death on December 6, 2020.